PUBLISHING

NUMERACY

Can-U-Cards

A creative approach to consolidating maths skills

BOOK 1

YEAR 4–6

Pauleen Novosel

Jason Novosel

Title: Numeracy CAN U CARDS
A creative approach to consolidating maths skills – Years 4–6: Book 1

Authors: Pauleen Novosel and Jason Novosel

Editor: Jennifer Clark

Designer: Freshfields Graphic Design

Book code: PB00106

ISBN: 978-1-908735-85-0

Published: 2012

Publisher: TTS Group Ltd

Park Lane Business Park
Kirkby-in-Ashfield
Notts, NG17 9GU
Tel: 0800 318 686
Fax: 0800 137 525

Websites: www.tts-shopping.com

About the authors: Pauleen Novosel has been teaching for more than 20 years in early childhood as well as being a music specialist, a relief teacher and a speech and drama teacher. Pauleen has taught in both private and state schools in Queensland, Australia, where she began her teaching career, as well as in the United Kingdom. With particular interests in literacy, early childhood and the arts, she has also been a guest speaker in literacy and has vast experience in curriculum planning and in the preparation and presentation of school-based documents for accreditation. Now enjoying her retirement, Pauleen continues her learning journey through travel and an interest in developing educational resources.

After beginning to teach in 1998 in a private secondary school in Queensland, Jason Novosel transitioned to the state secondary system as acting Head of Department English. Having gathered an array of teaching experiences and qualifications along the way, he has now launched his own training and consultancy business to pursue his passion for adult education. Jason has developed training and assessment units and has sat on district panels for curriculum subject development in Queensland. Jason shares his creative flair for designing educational materials with his mother and co-author, Pauleen.

Contents

Introduction 4

Curriculum links 4
What will students learn from Platform 2? 5
Why is numeracy so important? 6
How do I use the CAN U CARDS? 7

Numeracy CAN U CARDS and questions 10

Green 10
Yellow 24
Red 38

Suggested answers 54

Templates 58

CAN U CARD 58
Recording sheet 59
Tracking sheet 60

Introduction

Can you imagine stepping off the teach–test–record train to enjoy a fulfilling learning interaction with your class? The *Numeracy CAN U CARDS* series offers just that opportunity with an informal, short and exploratory method of assessing basic numeracy skills. Created to complement the teaching of mathematical concepts such as number facts, place value and number operations, these fun (yet purposeful) CAN U CARDS invite all of your students to practise their numeracy skills in a supportive environment.

CAN U CARDS are structured developmentally in two platforms:

- Platform 1 (Years 1-3) is designed for the needs of children through to Year 3.
- Platform 2 (Years 4-6) spans Years 4–6.

These cards can also be useful in secondary education, adult numeracy classes and for teaching English to speakers of other languages. Although a sample set of CAN U questions is supplied with each card for convenience, you also have the option of creating your own questions to shape the learning experience to the specific needs of your group of learners.

The self-explanatory, simple design of CAN U CARDS is a great strength for classroom use. Although they cover an expanse of opportunities for learning, practice and the development of mental acuity, they do not require onerous preparation or an extensive system of pre-testing and matching of cards with students. They also bring with them a relaxed creativity and explorative camaraderie, changing the mood of any classroom and introducing an easy flow of dialogue, ideas and opinions while still focusing on the essential elements of numeracy.

So sit back and relax with a CAN U CARD and let the numeracy practice begin.

Curriculum links

Given the generic nature of the numeracy skills, the cards are relevant to a broad range of learners. In terms of specific curriculum fit, CAN U CARDS are designed for:

- the number and algebra content of the United Kingdom curriculum, aligning to the *Primary Framework for Literacy and Mathematics, September 2006*
- the number and algebra content of the Australian curriculum, aligning to the 2010 draft standards of the Australian curriculum
- the number and algebra content of the New Zealand curriculum, aligning to the *New Zealand Curriculum 2007*.

What will students learn from Platform 2?

By the time they have completed Platform 2, students will have:

- practised mental and written strategies with one- and two-digit numbers
- worked with numbers including fractions and decimals to thousandths
- applied their place value understanding to establish equivalences
- used estimation strategies to predict and check reasonableness of calculations.

The chart outlines the specific learning objectives for each colour of the cards.

Mathematics concept	Green	Yellow	Red
Counting	Understand fractions as rational numbers (eg, counting by quarters, halves or with mixed numbers).		Order positive and negative integers.
Fractions	Use halves, thirds, quarters, fifths, eighths and tenths. Rename to find equivalent fractions. Solve problems involving fractions as operators.	Add and subtract fractions with the same or related denominators. Solve problems involving fractions as operators.	Use equivalency to compare and contrast fractions with unrelated denominators.
Decimals		Use and order numbers involving tenths and hundredths and connect them to fractions.	Use and order numbers with thousandths and connect them to fractions (eg, using technology).
Numeration	Recognise, represent, visualise and order numbers to 1 million.		
Number patterns	Copy, continue, create, describe and identify missing elements in large number patterns (eg, patterns resulting from doing two operations).		
Place value	Use place value to describe, partition and regroup large numbers.	Use place value to describe, partition and regroup decimal and large numbers.	
Factors and multiples	Use multiples of two, five, ten and find the factors of those numbers. Continue increasing and decreasing number sequences from any starting point.	Identify and describe the properties of numbers including factors, multiples and composites.	Identify and describe the properties of prime, composite and square numbers.
Multiplication and division	Understand and become fluent with the multiplication and related division facts of 2, 3, 5 and 10 extending to 4, 6, 8 and 9.	Solve multiplication problems with large numbers and divide by one-digit numbers.	Use multiplication and related division facts in mental and written strategies, and calculators to explain reasoning.
Calculation and estimation	Select, explain, justify and apply mental or written strategies and/or use calculators in situations involving addition, subtraction, multiplication (one- and two-digit numbers) and division by one-digit numbers without remainders.	Use estimation and rounding to check the reasonableness of answers.	Estimate outcomes of calculations involving decimal numbers and justify the reasonableness of answers.

Source: Adapted from Draft Australian Curriculum 2010

Why is numeracy so important?

Numeracy, along with literacy, provides the basics of any classroom education. Every subject area draws on these skills – even if it simply involves locating a page in a sequence of numbers. A pertinent illustration of the practical relevance of "getting the basics right" is the constant complaint from employers that they cannot find employees who are competent in spelling, vocabulary and sentence construction or who can function without a calculator.

During our careers in education (between us spanning a period of more than 50 years), we have been trained in, exposed to and engaged with a wide variety of learning methodologies for teaching the basics – from the traditionalist rote method of the mid 20th century to the pedagogies supporting theories of multiple intelligences and self-directed learning. Certainly we recognise that learning and teaching styles are fluid and influenced by society's current understanding of cognition and development – and we have practised the teaching strategies associated with modern educational psychology. At the same time, across the years it remains fundamental that learners need to master the basic knowledge of numbers (and words) before they can achieve self-actualisation in learning.[1]

CAN U CARDS therefore move learners towards more creative uses of mathematics by first offering them strong extrinsic motivation for learning numeracy in its basic forms. In essence, these cards inject diversity, enjoyment and collegial interaction into purposeful learning and practice activities that focus on mental acuity rather than drill.

10 good reasons to use CAN U CARDS

CAN U CARDS provide great opportunities to:

1. **practise** concepts as they occur in real life – randomly, not drilled and predictable
2. **discuss** concepts taught in previous lessons
3. **identify** mathematical exceptions
4. **use** minimal equipment in valuable learning experiences (individual whiteboards, class board and a calculator)
5. **promote** authentic mental acuity for all students
6. **adapt** information to suit the needs of your students
7. **acknowledge** extension students
8. **encourage** reluctant learners
9. **share** knowledge with valuable teacher and student interaction
10. **challenge** participants.

1 Abraham Maslow (1943) A theory of human motivation. *Psychological Review*, 50: 370–96; Theory into Practice, Conditions of learning (R Gagne), http://tip.psychology.org/gagne.html, accessed 24 February 2010.

How do I use the CAN U Cards?

In this book, Platform 2 CAN U CARDS are divided into three different colours: green (seven cards), yellow (seven cards) and red (eight cards). Each card is accompanied by a sample set of questions. Within this broad structure there is considerable versatility:

- As students move along from green to yellow to red, the mathematical content becomes more difficult. Within a certain colour, however, the card number does not reflect that same developmental progression. For example, Green Card 6 is easier than Yellow Card 1, but Red Card 5 isn't necessarily more difficult than Red Card 3. Within a colour, therefore, you may choose an order that suits the needs of your students and classroom programme.
- CAN U CARDS also lend themselves to differentiated classroom instruction. You can use CAN U CARDS as a whole class activity or with small groups, pairs and individuals. Depending on the abilities of your students, you may need to facilitate the discussions during the CAN U CARD sessions.
- CAN U CARDS have the versatility to be used either orally as mental exercises or in written form. If working with individual whiteboards, students can display a record of their thinking that the whole class or group can reflect on later.
- Activities are not limited to the sample CAN U questions provided. With the CAN U CARDS as a springboard, you can create your own questions designed with the specific needs of your group of learners in mind.

Just follow the simple preparation and teaching instructions on the next page and then let the numeracy CAN U CARD journey begin.

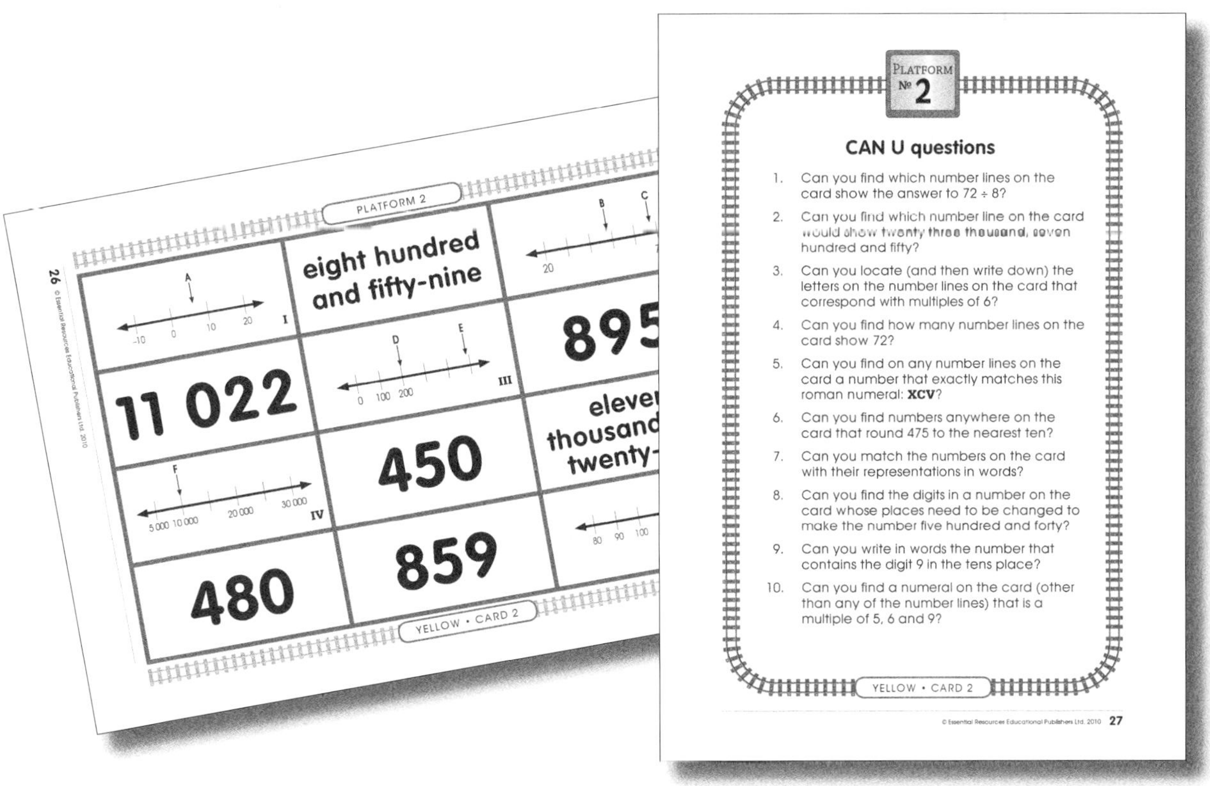

Preparing the CAN U CARDS

Note: These instructions apply only if you plan to use the cards with small groups, pairs or individuals. If you plan to practise these cards with the whole class, move straight to "Teaching with the CAN U CARDS". If you are preparing cards, we also recommend – in recognition of the many demands teachers have on their time – that you recruit parent volunteers or teaching assistants / teacher aides to help you with this stage.

1. If coloured copy paper is available, photocopy the CAN U CARDS on green, yellow and red paper. If coloured copy paper is not available, photocopy the CAN U CARDS on white paper and highlight or underline the card number with the designated colour. The number of copies you need to make of each card will depend on how you intend to use the cards.
2. Laminate the photocopied cards or use sheet protectors to make them more durable.
3. If you are using the "CAN U questions" sheets, photocopy as many copies as you need on white copy paper.
4. Laminate the photocopied question sheets or use sheet protectors to make them more durable.
5. If students are to record their answers on the Recording sheet template (p 59), photocopy as many copies as you need on white copy paper.

Teaching with the CAN U CARDS

Note: It is assumed that students have learnt the relevant numeracy concepts set out in the curriculum before they work with a CAN U CARD.

1. If you want the **whole class** to use the same card and set of questions, copy the CAN U CARD grid on a whiteboard, electronic whiteboard or overhead projector. Read the questions aloud to the students for them to answer (on individual whiteboards, orally, or in writing on the recording sheet template or in their notebooks).
2. If you want **small groups**, **pairs** or **individuals** to use different cards and sets of questions, prepare the cards as described above and then pass out the cards, questions and recording sheets (if using them). Students then record their answers on the recording sheet or in their notebook.
3. For **reluctant learners**, ask them to complete only a select number of questions, and don't impose a time limit. Regularly review and revisit the cards to help consolidate learning throughout the year. Also, if you have Book 1 of the series, you may use cards and questions from Platform 1, which are designed for lower year levels. It may also be helpful to review maths vocabulary ahead of time or allow students for instance to use a chart of roman numerals to assist in answering questions. Over time you may also find these learners gain confidence to actively contribute as they observe the open-endedness and diversity of answers.
4. For **extension students**, ask them to complete all of the questions in a certain amount of time. Challenge them to modify the CAN U CARDS to make them more difficult or give them copies of the CAN U CARD template to create new cards and questions for other classmates.

10 hints for working with CAN U CARDS

1. Card numbers within a colour set (green, yellow or red) do not reflect a developmental progression.
2. Revision and consolidation of concepts are inbuilt.
3. The design of multiple answers on each card allows learners to experience success, whether they provide a basic response or a more creative one.
4. Oral questioning facilitates the development of listening skills.
5. You may find it useful to break questions into parts according to the needs of your students.
6. The cards lend themselves to interactive e-learning sessions, in which information and communication technology (ICT) becomes integral to learning.
7. Questions expose learners to a diversity of subject-related vocabulary.
8. The cards can assist intervention for those students who have had difficulty with numeracy assessments.
9. It can be a valuable practice to repeat a card some weeks later to enable students to consolidate concepts and promote learning from peers. Revision can also encourage confident participation from students who have gleaned knowledge from the discussions generated by previous sessions.
10. It is not necessary to address all 10 questions on each card in one session, or even in the given order.

PLATFORM 2

6	13	19
5	12	17
4	6	9
9	8	8

GREEN • CARD 1

PLATFORM
№ 2

CAN U questions

1. Can you find two numbers and their total that is a double plus one on the card?
2. Can you find two even numbers and their total on the card?
3. Can you write the numbers in the column on the card that have the smallest total?
4. Can you make two subtraction number sentences whose answers are the same? All numbers used must be on the card.
5. Can you find a number on the card and its triple?
6. Can you find a row or column on the card that contains two numbers whose total is also on the same row or column?
7. Can you find a row on the card whose total is a prime number on the card?
8. Can you find the prime numbers on the card?
9. Can you find multiples of 2 on the card and add 500 to them?
10. Can you write an equation using at least 5 different numbers from the card?

GREEN • CARD 1

PLATFORM 2

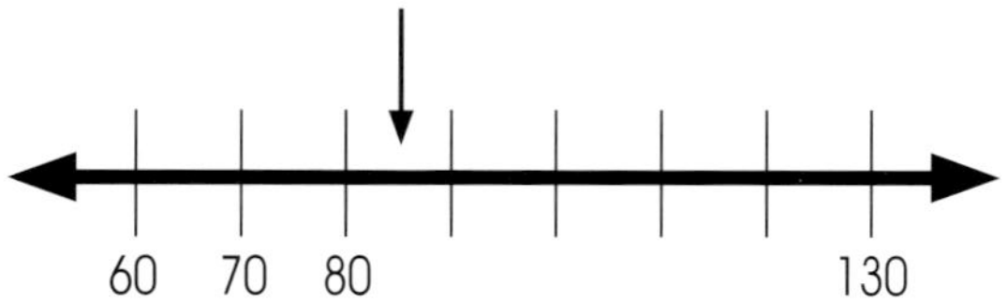

A

232

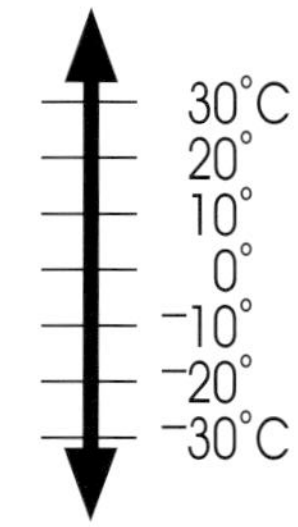

B

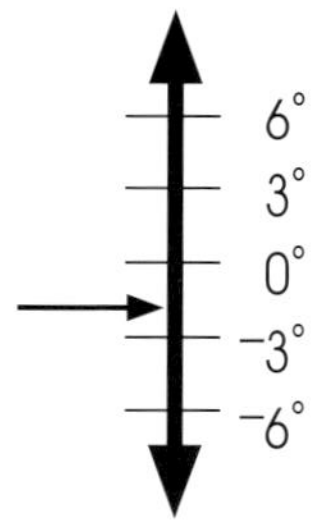

C

⁻2

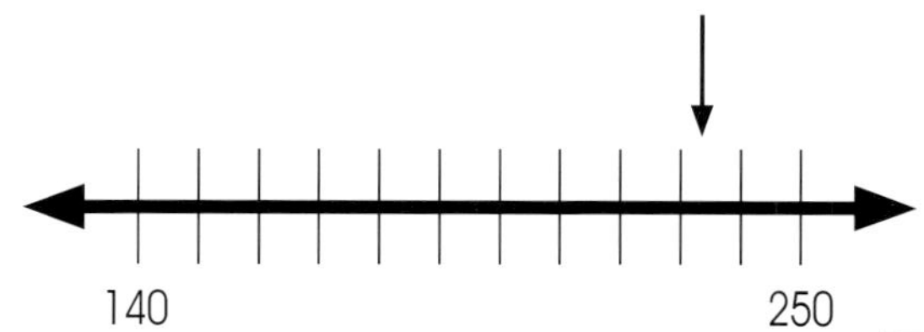

D

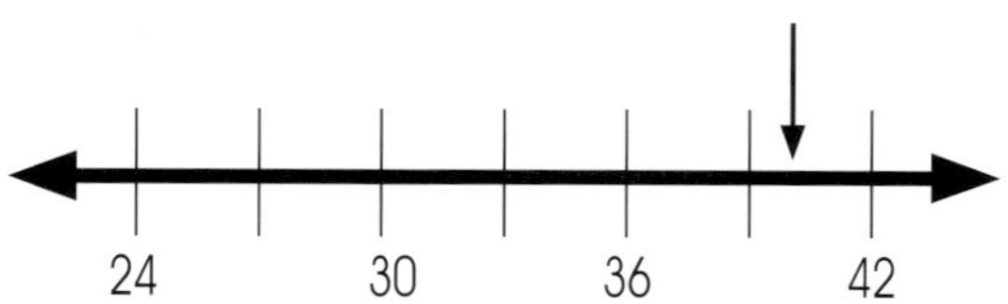

E

85

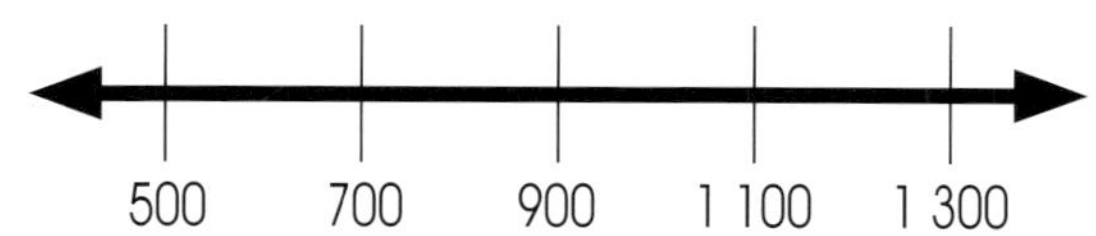

F

40

G

⁻4

GREEN • CARD 2

Platform № 2

CAN U questions

1. Can you match numbers on the card to their correct number lines on the card?
2. Can you combine two number lines on the card to make a new number line?
3. Can you find number lines on the card that show hops by 3?
4. Can you find how many number lines on the card show the number 25?
5. Can you find the number line on the card that would show a number that is double 85?
6. Can you find the number lines on the card where every interval is shown? Then, write the number that would appear halfway between each interval.
7. Can you find the number line on the card that shows the coldest temperature?
8. Can you find the number line on the card with the largest difference between the first and last numbers shown?
9. Can you write down the final numbers if each number line on the card was extended by five hops forward?
10. Can you write down the numbers each number line on the card would begin at if it was extended by 2 hops backward or downward?

GREEN • CARD 2

PLATFORM 2

60	35	36
399	30	420
81	18	9
5	79	64

GREEN • CARD 3

Platform № 2

CAN U questions

1. Can you find the square numbers on the card?
2. Can you find square numbers on the card that total 100?
3. Can you choose a number from the card and write all its factors?
4. Can you multiply a number on the card by the number of days in a week and find the answer on the card?
5. Can you find the numbers on the card whose total is closest to 500?
6. Can you find two numbers on the card whose difference is less than 20?
7. Can you find all the numerals on the card that have an even number in the tens place?
8. Can you add numbers on the card whose total would have zero in the ones place?
9. Can you find numbers and their halves or doubles on the card?
10. Can you estimate which row on the card would have the largest total?

GREEN • CARD 3

PLATFORM 2

2	10	0.8
11	?	17
28	20	15
12.2	110	2.8

GREEN • CARD 4

PLATFORM № 2

CAN U questions

1. Can you add numbers and find their totals on the card?
2. Can you suggest a number to fill the **?** to make its row on the card into a sequence with equal intervals?
3. Can you find a number on the card that is ten times larger than another number on the card?
4. Can you find the smallest number on the card?
5. Can you add one tenth to each number on the card?
6. Can you suggest a number to fill the **?** that would have something the same as all the other numbers in that column on the card?
7. Can you suggest a number to fill the **?** that would make the two middle rows on the card equal?
8. Can you choose a number from the card to write in words?
9. Can you triple three numbers on the card?
10. Can you find the number on the card that is greater than 0.8 and less than 2.8?

GREEN • CARD 4

PLATFORM 2

9	triple	6
24	halve	12
divide	64	4
14	2	double

GREEN • CARD 5

PLATFORM
№ 2

CAN U questions

1. Can you estimate which answer would be smaller – double 14 or triple 12?
2. Can you choose a word from the card that best describes how to get from 24 to 12?
3. Can you apply a word in a row of the card to the numbers on that row and give answers for your operations?
4. Can you divide the largest number on the card by the smallest number on the card?
5. Can you find numbers and their quotient on the card?
6. Can you find a number on the card that you could arrange in triangular form using dots?
7. Can you make an equation with only numbers on the card using a *x* sign, a + sign and an = sign?
8. Can you draw a number line to place three numbers on the card equal distances apart?
9. Can you find answers on the card for numbers on the card that can be both halved and tripled?
10. Can you find the row on the card that is all about multiples of three?

GREEN • CARD 5

PLATFORM 2

5 000	7	5 775
75	16	50 000
9	70 tens	13
21 012	25	50 hundreds

GREEN • CARD 6

Platform
№ 2

CAN U questions

1. Can you see 50 hundreds written another way on the card?
2. Can you combine other numbers on the card to make 5 775?
3. Can you find numbers on the card that have the same pattern of digits both forwards and backwards?
4. Can you estimate if 21 012 minus 5 775 would result in an odd or even number and use your calculator to test your answer?
5. Can you find the number on the card that the double of 21 012 would be closest to?
6. Can you find which numbers on the card are multiples of 5?
7. Can you find two-digit numbers on the card that are square numbers?
8. Can you use your calculator to compare 16 x 7 and 13 x 9? Show the comparison as a number sentence.
9. Can you find a number on the card ten times larger than another number on the card?
10. Can you arrange four numbers on the card in ascending order?

GREEN • CARD 6

PLATFORM 2

90	20	21
ninety one	1	1 000
?	twenty one	nineteen
twelve	fourteen	19

GREEN • CARD 7

Platform № 2

CAN U questions

1. Can you match words and numerals on the card?
2. Can you find a vowel letter that is missing from all the number words on the card?
3. Can you find a number on the card whose spelling includes the letter *a*? Write it in words.
4. Can you add a number written in words on the card to a numeral on the card to make the largest possible number?
5. Can you find two number words on the card that differ by two?
6. Can you use a calculator to total one half of the card?
7. Can you fill the **?** on the card with a numeral to make an evenly descending pattern across that row?
8. Can you recognise any numbers on the card that could be used to regroup another number on the card?
9. Can you place a number in the **?** on the card so that the pattern made by the top two numbers in that column is copied in the bottom half of the column?
10. Can you move across the card from left to right using only neighbouring numbers (including diagonals) made up of the digits 1 and 2? You can convert words to numerals where needed.

GREEN • CARD 7

PLATFORM 2

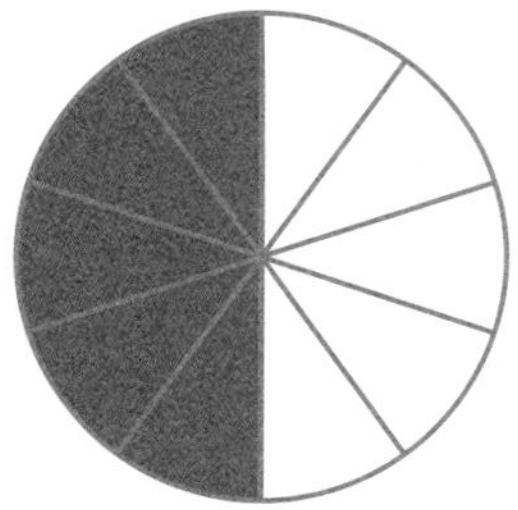		$\frac{25}{100}$
$\frac{3}{5}$	$\frac{5}{10}$	0.07
$\frac{7}{100}$	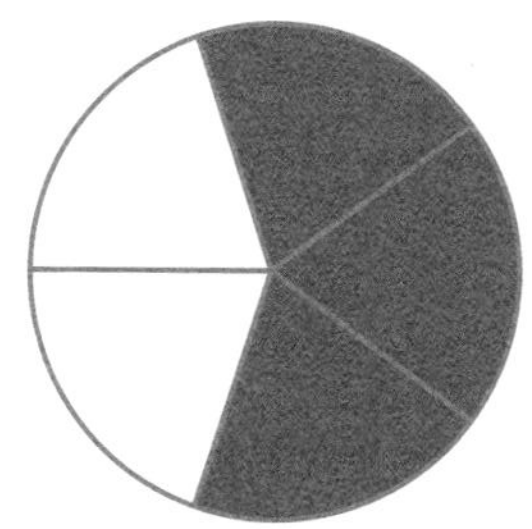	$\frac{1}{2}$
0.5	0.25	$\frac{1}{5}$

YELLOW • CARD 1

Platform № 2

CAN U questions

1. Can you match a picture on the card to its common fraction?
2. Can you find the picture that shows the sum of two common fractions on the card?
3. Can you find the common fractions on the card with denominators that are multiples of five?
4. Can you find the decimal fractions that match the common fractions on the card?
5. Can you find the common fraction on the card that is closest to one whole?
6. Can you find the smallest common fraction on the card?
7. Can you order the decimal fractions on the card from smallest to biggest?
8. Can you find a common fraction on the card that matches an unshaded portion of a picture on the card?
9. Can you find a picture to represent a decimal fraction on the card?
10. Can you use an appropriate mathematical sign (<, > or =) to compare two fractions on the card?

YELLOW • CARD 1

PLATFORM 2

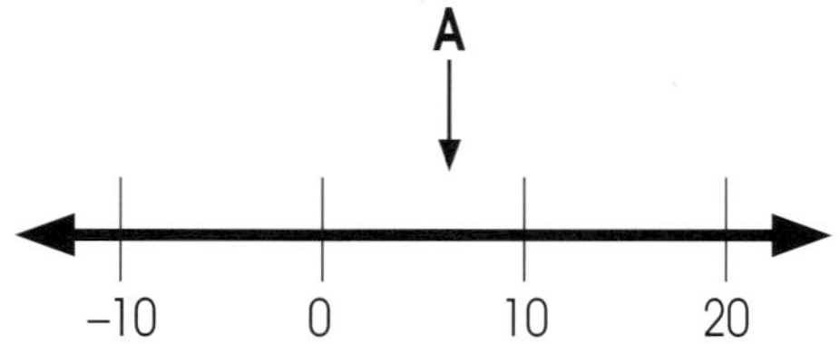 I	**eight hundred and fifty nine**	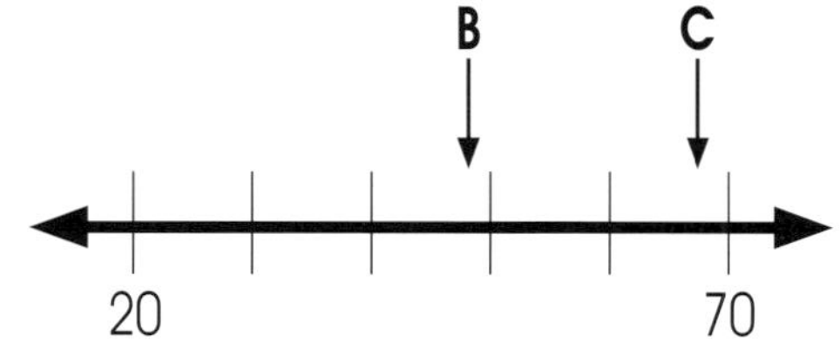 II
11 022	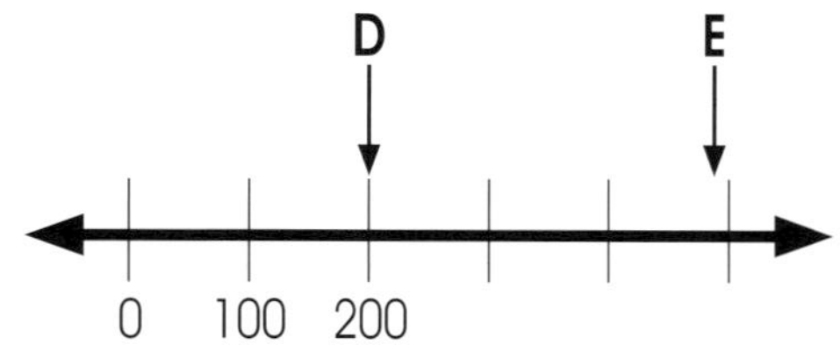 III	**895**
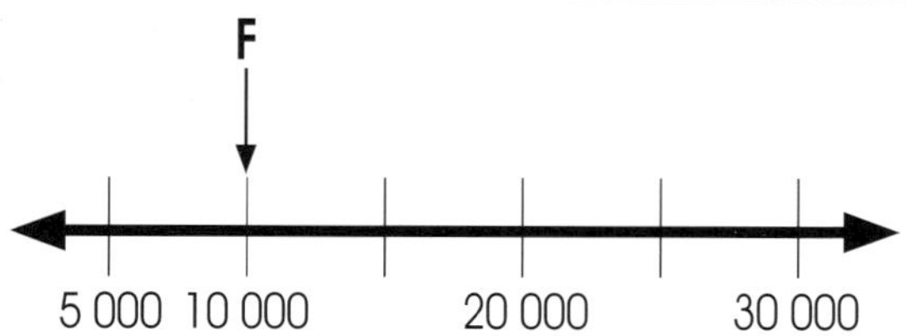 IV	**450**	**eleven thousand and twenty two**
480	**859**	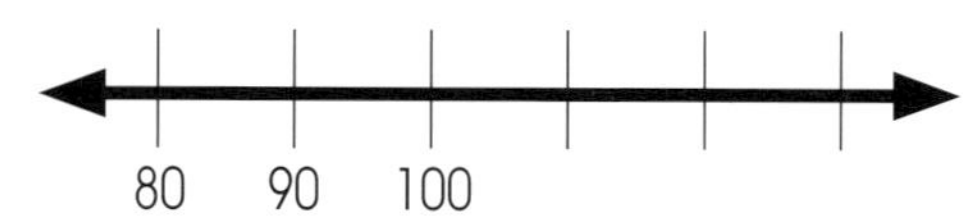 V

YELLOW • CARD 2

PLATFORM
№ 2

CAN U questions

1. Can you find which number lines on the card show the answer to 72 ÷ 8?
2. Can you find which number line on the card would show twenty three thousand, seven hundred and fifty?
3. Can you locate (and then write down) the letters on the number lines on the card that correspond with multiples of 6?
4. Can you find how many number lines on the card show 72?
5. Can you find on any number lines on the card a number that exactly matches this roman numeral: **XCV**?
6. Can you find numbers anywhere on the card that round 475 to the nearest ten?
7. Can you match the numbers on the card with their representations in words?
8. Can you find the digits in a number on the card whose places need to be changed to make the number five hundred and forty?
9. Can you write in words the number that contains the digit 9 in the tens place?
10. Can you find a numeral on the card (other than any of the number lines) that is a multiple of 5, 6 and 9?

YELLOW • CARD 2

PLATFORM 2

30	860	25
48	10	120
140	110	900
425	100	12

YELLOW • CARD 3

Platform № 2

CAN U questions

1. Can you find the number that is on the fourth row of the second column of the card?
2. Can you find a number on the card that is 25% of another number on the card?
3. Can you place a decimal point in a number on the card to make it the smallest number on the card?
4. Can you find numbers on the card that could be halved then added together to make 500?
5. Can you add two numbers on the card, double your total and find the answer on the card?
6. Can you add two numbers on the card, halve the total and find the answer on the card?
7. Can you find the number on the card to add to 110 to total another number on the card?
8. Can you write one tenth of each of the numbers on a row of the card?
9. Can you place three numbers on the card in a number pattern and add a number of your own in the pattern?
10. Can you divide 900 by a number on the card and find the answer on the card? (Your answer and number may be the same.)

YELLOW • CARD 3

PLATFORM 2

1 012	7	86 400
11	?	31
10%	28	50%
2 024	56	19

YELLOW • CARD 4

PLATFORM
№ 2

CAN U questions

1. Can you find prime numbers on the card that can be subtracted to make a multiple of 4?
2. Can you tell which numbers on the card could be evenly divided by 4? How can you tell?
3. Can you place a number in the **?** to make that row on the card total more than any other row on the card? You may use your calculator.
4. Can you fill in the **?** to make a number sequence going down that column on the card?
5. Can you compare two numbers on the card using 50% in your comparison?
6. Can you tell which number on the card you can find 10% of so that your answer is a whole number?
7. Can you add two numbers on the card and find a total that is a multiple of 7?
8. Can you add 10% of 86 400 to a multiple of 10 to make 8 700 or more?
9. Can you partition a four-digit number on the card into ones, tens, hundreds and thousands?
10. Can you identify a number on the card that is larger than 15 and smaller than 30?

YELLOW • CARD 4

PLATFORM 2

=	$\frac{6}{10}$	$\frac{1}{2}$
12	11	0.04
$\frac{4}{100}$	>	20
0.6	$\frac{6}{100}$	0.4

YELLOW • CARD 5

PLATFORM
№ 2

CAN U questions

1. Can you match common fractions on the card with decimal fractions on the card?
2. Can you arrange the common fractions on the card from largest to smallest?
3. Can you subtract a decimal fraction on the card from 1 and find the answer also on the card?
4. Can you find a fraction on the card that is ten times smaller than another fraction on the card?
5. Can you use a sign on the card to compare $\frac{1}{2}$ and 0.4?
6. Can you use four different numbers on the card to make an equation using the = sign?
7. Can you find a common fraction on the card that is equivalent to 0.5?
8. Can you make prime numbers by adding two-digit numbers on the card?
9. Can you add numbers on the card to reach a total that contains the numeral 1?
10. Can you arrange the decimal fractions on the card from smallest to largest?

YELLOW • CARD 5

PLATFORM 2

180	95	90
171	–	766
771	?	20
10 10 10 10 10 10 10 10 10	÷	9

YELLOW • CARD 6

Platform № 2

CAN U questions

1. Can you shade $\frac{1}{9}$ of the table at the bottom of the first column of the card?
2. Can you match the total number of tens shown in the table on the card to a numeral on the card?
3. Can you mark $\frac{1}{3}$ of the table on the card by circling it?
4. Can you find composite numbers on the card?
5. Can you write words that could be used to replace mathematical signs on the card?
6. Can you identify numbers on the card that differ by 5 and express this difference in an equation?
7. Can you choose a one-digit number to use with a three-digit number and a sign on the card to find an answer on the card?
8. Can you find numbers on the card with seven in the tens or hundreds place?
9. Can you fill the **?** with the difference between the two numbers on that row?
10. Can you find two numbers on the card that contain the same digits and write them in ascending order?

YELLOW • CARD 6

PLATFORM 2

4	7	3
9	5	4
1	6	2
3	8	7

YELLOW • CARD 7

PLATFORM
№ 2

CAN U questions

1. Can you place six different numbers on the card as digits to make the largest number?
2. Can you identify all the prime numbers on the card?
3. Can you show a rectangular number on the card by arranging it in an array of dots?
4. Can you square six numbers on the card?
5. Can you find the square root ($\sqrt{}$) of a number on the card?
6. Can you find which column on the card has the smallest total?
7. Can you find two numbers that are doubles plus one and multiply them?
8. Can you decrease each of the numbers in the second row by 0.5?
9. Can you increase numbers on the card by half their value and find the answers on the card?
10. Can you use the digits on the card to make equivalent fractions?

YELLOW • CARD 7

PLATFORM 2

396 223	121	369 232
17	3	41
369 200	9	3 136
⁻5	27	639 322

RED • CARD 1

PLATFORM
№ 2

CAN U questions

1. Can you use your calculator to find the product of 982 and 376? Check your answer and identify it on the card.
2. Can you find the numeral on the card that rounds your answer to question 1 to the nearest 100?
3. Can you sequence the six-digit numbers on the card from biggest to smallest?
4. Can you find the square numbers on the card? (You may need to use your calculator.)
5. Can you find the two-digit prime numbers on the card?
6. Can you find all the composite numbers on the card?
7. Can you find two integers on the card with a difference of eight?
8. Can you find the integers on the card that best fit on this number line?

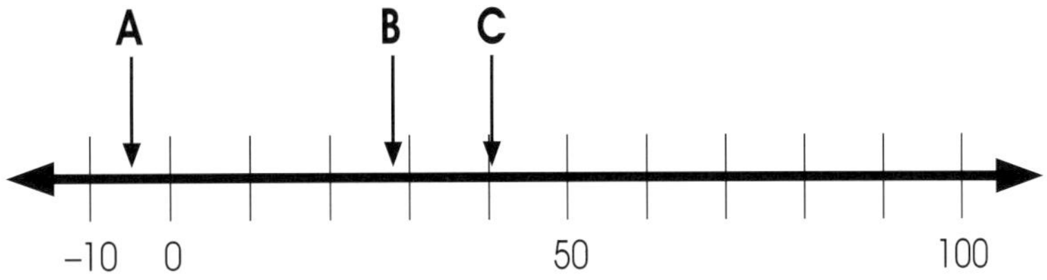

9. Can you find at least three numbers on the card to make an equation?
10. Can you find two numbers on the card with the product that is closest to 121?

RED • CARD 1

PLATFORM 2

0.5	100	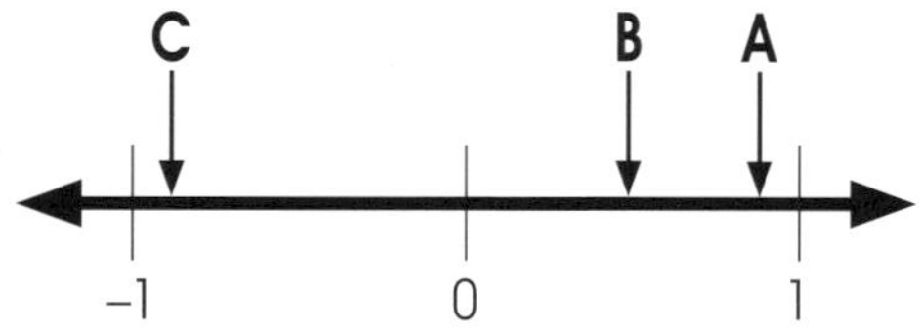 E
25%	$\frac{1}{4}$	2.25
$\frac{1}{2}$	0.9	90%
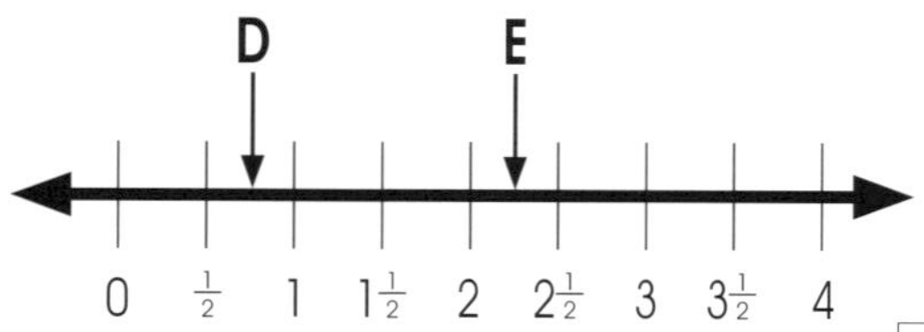 G	$\frac{9}{4}$	0.75

RED • CARD 2

Platform № 2

CAN U questions

1. Can you find which letters on the number lines match the decimal fractions on the card?
2. Can you see the same values expressed in different ways on the card?
3. Can you find decimal fractions on the card that have values in the hundredths place?
4. Can you find which number line would show the value of two common fractions on the card added together?
5. Can you add all the decimal fractions, round the answer to the nearest whole number and find it on a number line on the card?
6. Can you find the number line on the card that would show the result of 2.25 minus 0.5?
7. Can you write the number that each decimal fraction on the card (unless it is on a number line) would become if you multiplied it by the whole number on the card?
8. Can you find common denominators for the proper and improper fractions on the card?
9. Can you create an equation using three fractions on the card (decimal, proper and/or improper) that will have a total of 2?
10. Can you find the decimal fraction on the card that would combine with a common fraction on the card to make one whole?

RED • CARD 2

PLATFORM 2

16	8	121
5	100	$4 + (6 \times 2) = \square$
64	10	25
50	2	11

RED • CARD 3

PLATFORM
№ 2

CAN U questions

1. Can you find square numbers on the card and match them to their square roots on the card?
2. Can you identify the square numbers on the card that have only one prime number as a factor?
3. Can you find pairs of numbers on the card that have common factors?
4. Can you find a number that is a quarter of another number on the card?
5. Can you write equivalent fractions for one tenth using numbers from the card?
6. Can you use two numbers on the card to express a ratio and find another two numbers on the card to make an equivalent ratio?
7. Can you find the answer to the equation on the card?
8. Can you find numbers and their doubles on the card?
9. Can you find the average of the middle column on the card?
10. Can you write an equation using numbers on the card?

RED • CARD 3

PLATFORM 2

$\frac{25}{100}$	42	45.7
0.2	57	1.75
254.3	3.5	2
0.57	$\frac{22}{100}$	56.78

RED • CARD 4

PLATFORM
№ 2

CAN U questions

1. Can you find a fraction on the card to add to 56.78 to make a total on the card?
2. Can you make 300 using numbers on the card?
3. Can you find a number on the card whose digits could form a sequence increasing by one?
4. Can you make three numbers on the card (except the common fractions) ten times greater?
5. Can you find a number on the card that contains seven tenths?
6. Can you find a number on the card that is divided by 100 to make another number on the card?
7. Can you find numbers on the card that are multiples of 0.5?
8. Can you make the whole numbers on the card one hundred times smaller?
9. Can you change all the decimal numbers on the card into mixed numbers?
10. Can you arrange the numbers in a column on the card from largest to smallest?

RED • CARD 4

PLATFORM 2

90 000	99	one hundred and ten thousand
786	?	10 000
one hundred thousand	132	687
109 999	eleven	seven hundred and eighty six

RED • CARD 5

PLATFORM
№ 2

CAN U questions

1. Can you find a numeral on the card that is also written in words?
2. Can you find a number on the card (a word or a numeral) that is one larger than another number on the card?
3. Can you add two numbers on the card (words or numerals) and find their answer on the card?
4. Can you round the two-digit and three-digit numbers on the card to the nearest ten?
5. Can you find numbers on the card (numerals only) that are multiples of 3?
6. Can you fill the **?** with a square number that would fit in value between the other numbers on that row? (You may use your calculator.)
7. Can you find a way to make 9 from numbers on the card?
8. Can you find a common factor in a row or column on the card?
9. Can you find numbers on the card whose product or quotient is also on the card?
10. Can you fill the **?** with a number that has something in common with the rest of the column on the card?

RED • CARD 5

PLATFORM 2

22 966	392	47 034
<	949	70 000
98	8	x
23 517	–	49

RED • CARD 6

PLATFORM
№ 2

CAN U questions

1. Can you find numbers and their doubles on the card?
2. Can you use signs and numbers on the card to make an equation? (Your number and answer may be the same number from the card.)
3. Can you estimate which numbers on the card would make a total closest to 100 000? (Check with your calculator or use rounding.)
4. Can you list all the numbers on the card in descending order?
5. Can you find a number on the card that is a multiple of 7?
6. Can you find the number on the card with 7 in the thousands place?
7. Can you use the sign in a row on the card to write an equation using the numbers in that row? You may need to complete your equation with an answer.
8. Can you use numbers on the card and a sign on the card that would give an answer with only digits of 9 or 0?
9. Can you add numbers on the card whose total is less than 500?
10. Can you identify the value of three of the nines used in numbers on the card?

RED • CARD 6

PLATFORM 2

𝍸𝍸𝍸 𝍸𝍸 ǀǀǀ	0.25	80
XX	86	𝍸 ǀ
3 dozen	$\frac{1}{2}$	CD
1 century	200	6 dozen

RED • CARD 7

PLATFORM
№ 2

CAN U questions

1. Can you see the total on the card for a cricketer who scored twenty runs less than a century?
2. Can you find numbers on the card described in any form (including roman numerals and tallies) that would total 500?
3. Can you multiply each of three numbers on the card (in any form) by a fraction on the card and write your answers?
4. Can you identify the tally marks on the card that show how much larger eighty six is than eighty?
5. Can you find equivalent ratios using numbers expressed in any form on the card?
6. Can you write the numbers expressed in any form on a row of the card from largest to smallest?
7. Can you calculate the $\sqrt{}$ of a number on the card and find the answer on the card?
8. Can you find numbers on the card whose difference is half a century?
9. Can you double **XX** and give the answer in roman numerals?
10. Can you find numbers on the card in any form that could be used to express 25% as a decimal fraction or common fraction?

RED • CARD 7

PLATFORM 2

$1\frac{1}{2}$	$\frac{21}{10}$	15
$\frac{1}{2}$	5	$\frac{5}{6}$
18	$\frac{9}{7}$	$2\frac{3}{7}$
$\frac{1}{3}$	$2\frac{1}{10}$	6

RED • CARD 8

PLATFORM
№ 2

CAN U questions

1. Can you find the numeral on the card that would be the common denominator for two fractions on the card?
2. Can you say which fraction is larger, $\frac{1}{2}$ or $\frac{5}{6}$?
3. Can you find the product of a number on the card and a fraction on the card?
4. Can you use whole numbers on the card to make a fraction that is also expressed in its lowest possible terms on the card?
5. Can you match mixed numbers on the card to improper fractions on the card?
6. Can you total any amounts on the card that contain sevenths?
7. Can you find the whole number on the card that is not a multiple of 3?
8. Can you use numbers on the card to write an equation whose answer has 0 in the ones place?
9. Can you express $\frac{21}{10}$ as a decimal fraction?
10. Can you find two whole numbers on the card whose total or difference when added or subtracted is equal to the numerator of a fraction on the card?

RED • CARD 8

Suggested answers

Green Card 1 – Platform 2

1. 9 + 8 = 17, 13 + 4 = 17, 13 + 6 = 19, 12 + 5 = 17, 4 + 5 = 9
2. 6 + 6 = 12, 4 + 8 = 12
3. 6, 5, 4, 9
4. 17 – 9 = 8, 12 – 4 = 8; 12 – 8 = 4, 9 – 5 = 4, etc.
5. 4 × 3 = 12
6. 6 + 13 = 19, 12 + 5 = 17, 4 + 5 = 9, 8 + 9 = 17
7. 4, 6, 9 (19 is prime number)
8. 13, 19, 5, 17
9. 506, 512, 504, 508
10. 6 + 6 + 5 = 9 + 8, 6 + 5 + 8 = 13 + 6, 9 + 8 – 4 = 9 + 4, 8 + 8 + 17 = 4 × 5 + 13, etc.

Green Card 2 – Platform 2

1. A = 85, C = $^{-}2$, D = 232, E = 40. May also accept B = $^{-}2$ and/or $^{-}4$
2. A and D. Can also accept E and G
3. C, E, G
4. 2 (B, E)
5. D
6. B = $^{-}25$, $^{-}15$, $^{-}5$, 5, 15, 25; C = $^{-}4\frac{1}{2}$, $^{-}1\frac{1}{2}$, $1\frac{1}{2}$, $4\frac{1}{2}$; F = 600, 800, 1 000, 1 200
7. B
8. F
9. A = 140, 150, 160, 170, 180; B = 40°, 50°, 60°, 70°, 80°; C = 9°, 12°, 15°, 18°, 21°; D = 260, 270, 280, 290, 300; E = 45, 48, 51, 54, 57; F = 1 500, 1 700, 1 900, 2 100, 2 300; G = 1 287, 1 290, 1 293, 1 296, 1 299
10. A = 40, B = $^{-}50°$, C = $^{-}12°$, D = 120, E = 18, F = 100, G = 1 257

Green Card 3 – Platform 2

1. 36, 81, 64, 9
2. 36 + 64
3. Answers may vary. eg, 60 → 6, 10; 15, 4; 2, 30; 60, 1; 20, 3; 5, 12
4. **5** × 7 = **35**, **60** × 7 = **420**
5. 399 + 64 + 36, 420 + 81, 420 + 79, etc.
6. 36/35, 81/79, 79/64, 64/60, 30/18, 35/30, etc.
7. 60, 420, 81, 64
8. 81 + 79, 35 + 5, 81 + 64 + 5, 420 + 60, 36 + 64, 399 + 81, etc. (Discuss strategies.)
9. 60/30, 36/18, 9/18
10. 399, 30, 420 (Discuss strategies.)

Green Card 4 – Platform 2

1. 12.2 + 0.8 + 2 = 15, 2 + 0.8 = 2.8, 12.2 + 2.8 = 15, etc.
2. 14
3. 28/2.8, 110/11, 20/2
4. 0.8
5. 2.1, 10.1, 0.9, 11.1, 17.1, 28.1, 20.1, 15.1, 12.3, 110.1, 2.9
6. Any number ending in 0. Discuss strategies.
7. 35 (Discuss strategies.)
8. Answers may vary.
9. 3 × 2 = 6, 3 × 10 = 30, 3 × 11 = 33, 3 × 0.8 = 2.4, etc.
10. 2

Green Card 5 – Platform 2

1. double 14 (Discuss with students.)
2. divide (discuss why 'double' is not the best choice). Accept halve.
3. row 1: triple 9 = 27, triple 6 = 18; row 2: halve 24 = 12, halve 12 = 6; row 3: divide 64 (by) 4 = 16; row 4: double 14 = 28, double 2 = 4
4. 64 ÷ 2 = 32
5. 24 ÷ 2 = 12, 12 ÷ 2 = 6, 12 ÷ 6 = 2, 24 ÷ 4 = 6, etc.
6. 6 
7. 2 × 9 = 14 + 4, 9 × 4 = 24 + 12, 24 + 4 = 2 × 14, etc.
8. 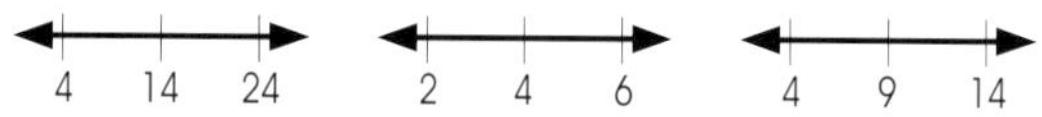

9. 4 halved = 2, 4 tripled = 12
10. 9, triple, 6 (Discuss with students.)

Green Card 6 – Platform 2

1. 5 000
2. 5 000 + 70 tens + 75; 50 hundreds + 70 tens + 75
3. 5 775, 21 012
4. Yes (odd number). Discuss strategies.
5. 50 000 (Discuss strategies.)
6. All the numbers which have 5 or 0 in the ones place (including 70 tens and 50 hundreds)
7. 16, 25
8. 13 × 9 > 16 × 7, 16 × 7 ≠ 13 × 9, 16 × 7 < 13 × 9
9. 50 000/5 000
10. Answers may vary. (eg, 7, 9, 13, 16 or 5 000, 5 775, 21 012, 50 000)

Green Card 7 – Platform 2

1. nineteen/19, twenty one/21
2. a
3. one thousand
4. 1 091
5. twelve/fourteen, nineteen/twenty one
6. Answers may vary. (eg, 2 rows of the card, alternate boxes, etc.) Discuss strategies.
7. **23**, 21, 19
8. 90 + 1 = 91, 20 + 1 = 21, 20 = 19 + 1
9. 11 (one less than 12)
10. twelve/twenty one/1/21

Yellow Card 1 – Platform 2

1. 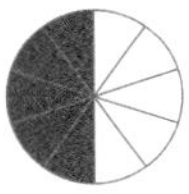 $= \frac{1}{2} = \frac{5}{10}$, 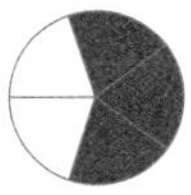 $= \frac{3}{5}$
2. $\frac{3}{5} + \frac{1}{5} =$ 
3. $\frac{3}{5}, \frac{1}{5}, \frac{5}{10}, \frac{25}{100}, \frac{7}{100}$
4. $\frac{7}{100} = 0.07$, $\frac{25}{100} = 0.25$, $\frac{5}{10} = 0.5$, etc.
5. $\frac{3}{5}$
6. $\frac{7}{100}$
7. 0.07, 0.25, 0.5
8. $\frac{1}{5}, \frac{1}{2}$
9. 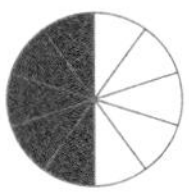 = 0.5
10. Answers may vary.

Yellow Card 2 Platform 2

1. I, III
2. IV
3. A(6), B(48), E(480)
4. 2 (II, III)
5. V (95)
6. 480 (III)
7. 859, 11 022
8. 450
9. eight hundred and ninety five
10. 450

Yellow Card 3 – Platform 2

1. 100
2. 12 is 25% of 48, 25 is 25% of 100, 30 is 25% of 120
3. 0.10 or 0.100
4. 860/140 (430 + 70), 900/100 (450 + 50)
5. 48 + 12 = 60 (doubled is 120), 425 + 25 = 450 (doubled is 900)
6. 140 + 100 = 240 (half is 120), 48 + 12 = 60 (half is 30)
7. 110 + 10 = 120; 110 + 30 = 140
8. 3, 86, 2.5; 4.8, 1, 12; 14, 11 90; 42.5, 10, 1.2
9. 110, 120, **130**, 140; 100, 110, 120, **130**; 100, 120, 140, **160**, etc.
10. 900 ÷ 30 = 30

Yellow Card 4 – Platform 2

1. 19 – 11 = 8, 31 – 7 = 24
2. 86 400, 2 024, 56, 28. Discuss strategies.
3. Answers may vary. Discuss strategies.
4. 14
5. 28 is 50% of 56, 1 012 is 50% of 2 024, 7 > 50% of 11, etc.
6. 86 400. Discuss.
7. 28 + 56 = 84, 11 + 31 = 42, 56 + 7 = 63, etc.
8. 8 640 + 60 = 8 700. Can also add any multiples of 10 above 60.
9. 1 012 = 1 000 + 10 + 2, 2 024 = 2 000 + 20 + 4, 86 400 = 80 000 + 6 000 + 400
10. 28 or 19

Yellow Card 5 – Platform 2

1. $\frac{6}{10}$ /0.6, $\frac{4}{100}$/0.04
2. $\frac{6}{10}, \frac{1}{2}, \frac{6}{100}, \frac{4}{100}$
3. 1 – 0.6 = 0.4, 1 – 0.4 = 0.6
4. $\frac{6}{100}$ / $\frac{6}{10}$, 0.04/0.4, $\frac{6}{100}$ /0.6, etc.
5. $\frac{1}{2} > 0.4$
6. 12 – 11 = 0.6 + 0.4; 11 + 0.4 + 0.6 = 12; ($\frac{6}{10} - \frac{1}{2} = \frac{4}{100} + \frac{6}{100}$ extension)
7. $\frac{1}{2}$
8. 12 + 11 = 23, 20 + 11 = 31
9. Answers may vary. (eg, 20 + 11 = 31, $\frac{4}{100} + \frac{6}{100} = \frac{10}{100}$ (or 0.1))
10. 0.04, 0.4, 0.6

Yellow Card 6 – Platform 2

1. Shading may vary.

10	10	10
10	10	10
10	10	10

2. 9 or 90
3. Circling may vary.

10	10	10
10	10	10
10	10	10

4. 90, 9, 180, 766, 771, 171, 20, 95
5. minus, take away, divided by, shared between
6. 95 – 90 = 5, 771 – 766 = 5, 90 + 95 – 180 = 5
7. 180 ÷ 9 = 20, 180 – 9 = 171
8. 171, 766, 771
9. 751
10. 171, 771

Yellow Card 7 – Platform 2

1. 98 7654
2. 2, 3, 5, 7
3. 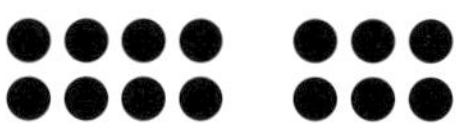
4. Answers may vary. (eg, $9^2 = 81$, $4^2 = 16$)
5. $\sqrt{9} = 3$, $\sqrt{4} = 2$, $\sqrt{1} = 1$
6. 3rd column
7. 3 × 3 = 9, 9 × 5 = 45, 5 × 3 = 15, 7 × 5 = 35, 9 × 7 = 63, 3 × 7 = 21, 7 × 7 = 49
8. 8.5, 4.5, 3.5
9. 2 + 1 = 3, 4 + 2 = 6, 6 + 3 = 9
10. $\frac{3}{4} = \frac{6}{8}$, $\frac{3}{6} = \frac{2}{4} = \frac{1}{2}$, $\frac{4}{6} = \frac{2}{3}$, $\frac{1}{4} = \frac{2}{8}$, etc.

Red Card 1 – Platform 2

1. 369 232
2. 369 200
3. 639 322, 396 223, 369 232, 369 200
4. 3 136, 121, 9
5. 17, 41
6. 121, 9, 27, 369 232, 369 200, 639 322, 3 136
7. $^-5$ and 3, 9 and 17
8. A = $^-5$, B = 27, C = 41
9. 3 × 27 = 9^2, 27 + 17 = 41 + 3, 17 – 3 = 41 – 29, 3 × 9 = 27, 369 232 – 369 200 + 9 = 41, $\sqrt{121}$+ 9 = 17 + 3, etc.
10. 3 × 41

Red Card 2 – Platform 2

1. A = 0.9, B = 0.5, D = 0.75, E = 2.25
2. 0.9 and 90%, 2.25 and $\frac{9}{4}$, 0.5 and $\frac{1}{2}$, $\frac{1}{4}$ and 25%
3. 0.75, 2.25
4. Both number lines E and G. $\frac{3}{4} = \frac{1}{4} + \frac{1}{2}$, $2\frac{1}{2} = \frac{1}{4} + \frac{9}{4}$, $2\frac{3}{4} = \frac{1}{2} +$
5. 4.4 rounds to 4 on number line G.
6. 1.75 on number line G.
7. 50, 225, 90, 75
8. 4, 8, 12, 16, etc.
9. $\frac{9}{4} - \frac{1}{2} + \frac{1}{4} = 2$
10. $0.5 + \frac{1}{2} = 1$, $0.75 + \frac{1}{4} = 1$

Red Card 3 – Platform 2

1. $\sqrt{121} = 11$, $\sqrt{64} = 8$, $\sqrt{100} = 10$, $\sqrt{25} = 5$
2. 121 (11 × 11), 25 (5 × 5), 64 (2 × 2 × 2 × 2 × 2 × 2)
3. 100/25, 64/100, 8/100, 8/64, etc.
4. 25/100, 16/64, 2/8
5. $\frac{5}{50}$, $\frac{10}{100}$
6. 8:16/25:50, 50:100/8:16, 25:100/16:64, 25:100/2:8, etc.
7. 16 (Discuss order of operations.)
8. 50/100, 8/6, 25/50, 5/10
9. (8 + 100 + 10 +2) ÷ 4 = 30
10. 121 + 10 + 2 = 2 × 10 + 100 +8 + 5, 2 × 50 = 100, 2 × 5 = 10, 100 ÷ 5 = 2 × 10, etc.

Red Card 4 – Platform 2

1. $\frac{22}{100} + 56.78 = 57$
2. 254.3 + 45.7 = 300, 254.3 + 3.5 + 0.2 + 42 = 300
3. 56.78, 254.3
4. 420, 457, 2, 570, 17.5, 2 543, 35, 20, 5.7, 567.8
5. 45.7, 1.75, 56.78
6. 57 ÷ 100 = 0.57
7. 42, 57, 3.5, 2
8. 0.42, 0.57, 0.02
9. $45\frac{7}{10}$, $\frac{2}{10}$, $1\frac{75}{100}$, $254\frac{3}{10}$, $3\frac{5}{10}$, $\frac{57}{100}$, $56\frac{78}{100}$
10. 254.3, 0.57, $\frac{25}{100}$, 0.2;

    57, 42, 3.5, $\frac{22}{100}$;

    56.78, 45.7, 2, 1.75

Red Card 5 – Platform 2

1. Seven hundred and eighty six = 786
2. One hundred and ten thousand >109 999
3. One hundred thousand + 10 000 = one hundred and ten thousand, 687 + 99 = 786, 90 000 + 10 000 = one hundred thousand
4. 790, 100, 690, 130, may except ten
5. 99, 786, 687, 90 000
6. 8 100 (90^2), 4900 (70^2), etc. Numbers between 29^2 and 99^2.
7. 90 000 ÷ 10 000 = 9, 99 ÷ 11 = 9
8. 11 (99, 132, eleven), 2 (786, 10 000)
9. 11 × 10 000 = one hundred and ten thousand, or One hundred and ten thousand ÷ 11 = 10 000
10. Any multiple of 11. Discuss any other strategies.

Red Card 6 – Platform 2

1. 23 517/47 034, 49/98
2. 70 000 – 47 034 = 22 966, 98 – 49 = 49, 98 < 949, 47 034 – 23 517 = 23 517, 49 × 8 = 392, etc.
3. 70 000 + 23 517 + 949 + 392+ 98, etc. Discuss strategies.
4. 70 000, 47 034, 23 517, 22 966, 949, 392, 98, 49, 8
5. 49, 98, 70 000, 392
6. 47 034
7. 949 < 70 000, 98 × 8 = 784, 23 517 – 49 = 23 468
8. 949 – 49 = 900, 98 – 8 = 90
9. 98 + 8, 49 + 98, 392 + 49, etc.
10. 9, 90, 900

Red Card 7 – Platform 2

1. 80
2. 6 dozen + 𝍸𝍸𝍸𝍸𝍸𝍷𝍷𝍷 + **CD** = 500, **CD** + 1 century = 500, **CD** + 80 + **XX** = 500
3. Answers may vary. (eg $\frac{1}{2}$ of 28 = 14, $\frac{1}{2}$ × **CD** = 200, 80 × 0.25 = 20, **XX** × 0.25 = 5, **CD** × 0.25 = 100)
4. 𝍸𝍷
5. 3 dozen:6 dozen/ 200:**CD**/ 1 century:200
6. 80 / 𝍸𝍸𝍸𝍸𝍸𝍷𝍷𝍷 / 0.25, 86 / **XX** / 𝍸𝍷, **CD**, 3 dozen, $\frac{1}{2}$, 200/ 1 century / 6 dozen
7. √**CD** = **XX**, √3 dozen = 𝍸𝍷
8. 86 – 3 dozen = 50
9. **XL**
10. 0.25, $\frac{\textbf{XX}}{80}$, $\frac{\text{1 century}}{\textbf{CD}}$

Red Card 8 – Platform 2

1. 6 ($\frac{1}{3}$ and $\frac{1}{2}$, $\frac{5}{6}$ and $\frac{1}{3}$, $\frac{5}{6}$ and $\frac{1}{2}$) 18 ($\frac{1}{3}$ and $\frac{5}{6}$)
2. $\frac{5}{6}$
3. $\frac{1}{3}$ × 18 = 6, $\frac{5}{6}$ × 18 = 15, $\frac{1}{3}$ × 15 = 5
4. $\frac{5}{6}$ as $\frac{5}{6}$, $\frac{15}{18}$ expressed as $\frac{5}{6}$, $\frac{15}{18}$ expressed as $\frac{1}{3}$, $\frac{5}{15}$ expressed as $\frac{1}{3}$
5. $\frac{21}{10}$ / $2\frac{1}{10}$
6. $3\frac{5}{7} = \frac{9}{7} + 2\frac{3}{7}$
7. 5
8. 15 – 5 = 10, 6 × 5 = 30, 5 × 18 = 90, $\frac{1}{3}$ × 15 – 5 = 0, (18 ÷ 6) – (15 ÷ 5) = 0, $\frac{1}{2}$ × (15 + 5) = 10, etc. Discuss strategies.
9. 2.1
10. 15 + 6 = $\frac{(21)}{10}$, 15 – 6 = $\frac{(9)}{7}$, 18 – 15 = $\frac{(3)}{7}$, 6 – 5 = $\frac{(1)}{2}$ or $\frac{(1)}{10}$ Discuss *numerator*.

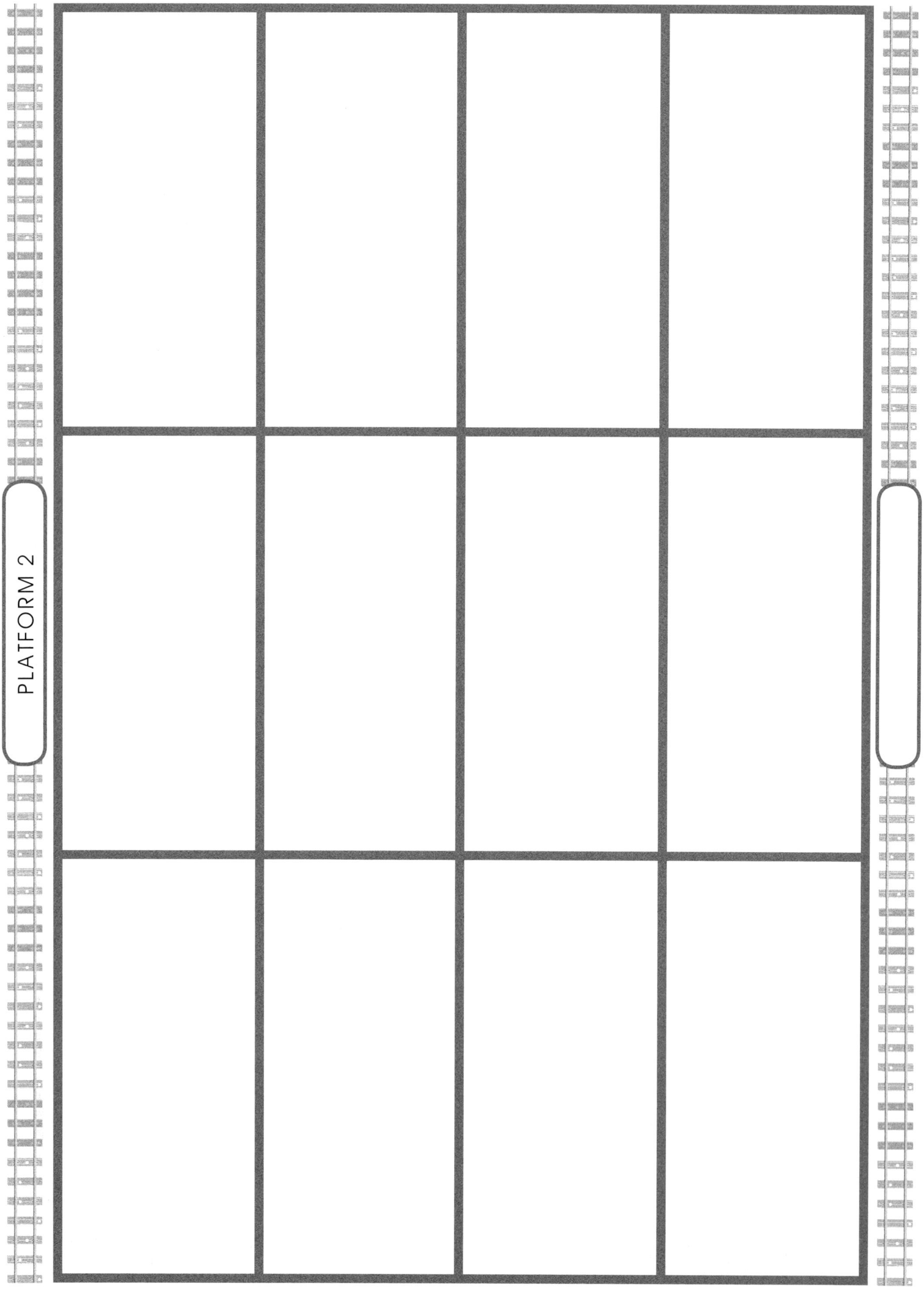
PLATFORM 2

PLATFORM
№ 2

Name:

Date:

Recording sheet

1.

2.

3.

4.

5.

6.

7.

8.

9.

10.

PLATFORM
№ 2

Tracking sheet

Student	Green							Yellow							Red							
	1	2	3	4	5	6	7	1	2	3	4	5	6	7	1	2	3	4	5	6	7	8

